Phonemic Awareness Songs and Rhymes

by Wiley Blevins

NEW YORK • TORONTO • LONDON • AUCKLAND • SYDNEY
MEXICO CITY • NEW DELHI • HONG KONG • BUENOS AIRES

Teaching *Resources*

Credits:

"Birds' Square Dance" by Beverly McLoughland, first appeared in RANGER RICK, 1988.
Author controls all rights.

"Dance" from HIGGLE WIGGLE by Eve Merriam. Copyright © 1994 by the Estate of
Eve Merriam by Marian Reiner, Literary Executor. Reprinted by permission of Marian Reiner.

"100 Is a Lot!" by Meish Goldish. From A POEM A DAY © 1997 Scholastic Inc.

"Pin Pón" from, WEE SING AROUND THE WORLD by Pamela Conn Beall and Susan Hagen Nipp
with Nancy Spence Klein. Copyright © 1994 by Pamela Conn Beall and Susan Hagen Nipp.
Published by Price Stern Sloan, Inc. A member of The Putnam & Grosset Group, New York, NY.

"Six Little Ducks" from THE FIRESIDE BOOK OF CHILDREN'S SONGS collected and edited by
Marie Winn. Copyright © 1966 Marie Winn and Allan Miller; copyright renewed 1994 Marie
Winn and Allan Miller. Reprinted with permission of Little Simon, an imprint of Simon &
Schuster Children's Publishing Division.

SING by Joe Raposo copyright © 1971 (Renewed) Jonico Music, Inc. All Rights Reserved.
Used by permission of WARNER BROS. PUBLICATIONS. U.S. Inc., Miami, FL. 33014

"Wonderful World" by Eva Grant. From POETRY PLACE ANTHOLOGY.
Copyright © 1983 by Edgell Communications, Inc. First Scholastic printing, 1990.

"Vacuum Cleaner" by Ethel Jacobson. From A POEM A DAY. Copyright © 1997 Scholastic, Inc.

"Willoughby Wallaby Woo" from ALLIGATOR PIE (Macmillan of Canada, 1974).
Copyright © 1974 Dennis Lee. With permission of the author.

"Chicken Pox" by Terry Cooper. From A POEM A DAY copyright © 1997 Scholastic Inc.

Audio Credits:

Produced by A Gentle Wind, Albany, NY.

All songs performed by Bob Van Detta (guitar, bass, vocals), Linda Schrade (vocals),
Seana Munson (vocals), David Kiphuth (banjo, vocals), John Kirk (fiddle), and Brian Mellick
(percussion), except where noted.

All songs arranged by Jill and Donald Person, Paul Strausman, and Bob Van Detta, except where noted.

Children's Chorus: Deborah Rose Chesser, Allison Kiphuth, Arlen Strausman, Raina Strausman,
Shea Strausman, and Kyle Turin.

Note:
"Sing!" (additional vocals by Kim Harris, Amanda Aldi, Stephen Jones, and Jennifer Stewart).

"Willoughby, Wallaby, Woo" (arranged and performed by Reggie's Redhot Feetwarmers).

"Five Little Fishies" (read by Marcia Lane).

"Jack Be Nimble" (vocals by Paul Strausman).

Cover design by Mo Bing Chan
Cover illustration by Ramune Jauniskis
Interior design by Solutions by Design, Inc.
Illustration by Nicholas B. Lamia and Maxie Chambliss

Product ISBN 0–439–66114–5
Book ISBN 0–439–66116–1

Contents

What Is Phonemic Awareness?

The two best predictors of early reading success are alphabet recognition and phonemic awareness. —Marilyn Jager Adams

When I became a teacher, the term *phonemic awareness* was never uttered. However, during that first year I began to notice children who struggled learning how words "work." That is, they seemed to have difficulty mapping sounds to spellings, blending sounds to decode words, and even understanding that words are made up of different sounds. I searched for ways to address my students' needs, but with varied success. Now, years later, I have learned that one important piece of the "reading puzzle" I was missing was phonemic awareness. Some of my students lacked this essential skill and there was much I could have done to help them. As I travel around the country conducting phonemic awareness workshops, I encounter many teachers searching for answers to the same questions I had. *What is phonemic awareness? Why is it important? How do you teach it?* This book addresses those questions.

Phonemic awareness is the understanding or insight that a word is made up of a series of discrete sounds (phonemes). This awareness includes the ability to pick out and manipulate sounds in spoken words. A related term, sometimes confused with phonemic awareness, is **phonological awareness.** Phonological awareness is an "umbrella" term that includes phonemic awareness, or awareness of words at the phoneme (sound) level. It also includes an awareness of word units larger than the phoneme. Therefore, phonological awareness includes:

- words within sentences;
- rhyming units within words;
- beginning and ending sounds within words;
- syllables within words;
- phonemes, or sounds, within words (phonemic awareness); and
- features of individual phonemes such as how the mouth, tongue, vocal cords, and teeth are used to produce the sound.

Phonemic awareness is not the same thing as phonics. Phonemic awareness deals with sounds in spoken words, whereas phonics involves the relationship between sounds and written symbols. Therefore, phonics deals with learning sound-spelling relationships and is associated with print. Most phonemic awareness tasks, by contrast, are purely oral.

According to Adams (1990), there are **five basic types of phonemic awareness tasks.** Within each task type are progressively more complex activities. Although some of the tasks are more accurately labeled phonological awareness tasks, the goal of most tasks is awareness at the phoneme level. These task types and sample activities include the following:

TASK 1—
The ability to hear rhymes and alliteration

a. rhyme *Example:* I once saw a <u>cat</u>, sitting next to a <u>dog</u>. I once saw a <u>bat</u>, sitting next

---

KEY TERMS

Before using the poems, songs, and activities provided, familiarize yourself with the following terms used throughout the book.

onset: refers to the part of the syllable that comes before the vowel. An onset can be a single consonant, consonant cluster, or consonant digraph. (For example, the letter *c* in *cat*, the letters *pl* in *plate*, and the letters *ch* in *chair*.)

rime: a vowel and any consonants that follow it in a syllable. (For example, the letters *at* in the word *cat*.)

phoneme: a sound; the smallest unit of speech sound that distinguishes one word from another in a language.

to a <u>frog</u>.

b. **alliteration** *Example:* <u>S</u>ix <u>s</u>nakes <u>s</u>ell <u>s</u>odas and <u>s</u>nacks.

c. **assonance** *Example:* The l<u>ea</u>f, the b<u>ea</u>n, the p<u>ea</u>ch—all were within r<u>ea</u>ch.

TASK 2—
The ability to do oddity tasks

a. **rhyme** *Example:* Which word does not rhyme: *cat, sat, pig*? (pig)

b. **beginning consonants** *Example:* Which two words begin with the same sound: *man, sat, sick*? (sat, sick)

c. **ending consonants** *Example:* Which two words end with the same sound: *man, sat, ten*? (man, ten)

d. **medial sounds (long vowels)** *Example:* Which word does not have the same middle sound: *take, late, feet*? (feet)

e. **medial sounds (short vowels)** *Example:* Which two words have the same middle sound: *top, cat, pan*? (cat, pan)

f. **medial sounds (consonants)** *Example:* Which two words have the same middle sound: *kitten, missing, lesson*? (missing, lesson)

TASK 3—
The ability to orally blend words

a. **syllables** *Example:* Listen to these word parts. Say the word as a whole. *ta...ble*—What's the word? (table)

b. **onset/rime** *Example:* Listen to these word parts. Say the word as a whole. */p/...an*—What's the word? (pan)

c. **phoneme by phoneme** *Example:* Listen to these word parts. Say the word as a whole. /s/ /a/ /t/—What's the word? (sat)

TASK 4—
The ability to orally segment words (including counting sounds)

a. **syllables** *Example:* Listen to this word: *table*. Say it syllable by syllable. (ta...ble)

b. **onset/rime** *Example:* Listen to this word: *pan*. Say the first sound in the word (the onset) and then the rest of the word (the rime). (/p/...an)

c. **phoneme by phoneme (counting sounds)** *Example:* Listen to this word: *sat*. Say the word sound by sound. (/s/ /a/ /t/) How many sounds do you hear? (3)

TASK 5—
The ability to do phonemic manipulation tasks

a. **initial sound substitution** *Example:* Replace the first sound in *mat* with /s/. (sat)

b. **final sound substitution** *Example:* Replace the last sound in *mat* with /p/. (map)

c. **vowel substitution** *Example:* Replace the middle sound in *map* with /o/. (mop)

d. **syllable deletion** *Example:* Say *baker* without the *ba*. (ker)

e. **initial sound deletion** *Example:* Say *sun* without the /s/. (un)

f. **final sound deletion** *Example:* Say *hit* without the /t/. (hi)

g. **initial phoneme in a blend deletion** *Example:* Say *step* without the /s/. (tep)

h. **final phoneme in a blend deletion** *Example:* Say *best* without the /t/. (bes)

i. **second phoneme in a blend deletion** *Example:* Say *frog* without the /r/. (fog)

Why Is Phonemic Awareness Important?

Children sometimes come to school unaware that words consist of a series of discrete sounds. Phonemic awareness activities help children learn to distinguish individual sounds, or phonemes, within words. This awareness is a prerequisite skill for children learning to associate sounds with letters and manipulating sounds to blend words (during reading) or segment words (during spelling). "It is unlikely that children lacking phonemic awareness can benefit fully from phonics instruction since they do not understand what letters and spellings are supposed to represent." (Juel, Griffith, & Gough, 1986)

Often children who have difficulties with phonics instruction do so because they have not developed the prerequisite phonemic awareness skills that many children gain through years of exposure to rhymes, songs, and being read to. **Phonemic awareness training provides the foundation on which phonics instruction is built.** "Children who begin school with little phonemic awareness will have trouble acquiring the alphabetic principle which will, in turn, limit their ability to decode words" (Ball & Blachman, 1991).

Research indicates that approximately 20% of children are affected by a lack of phonemic awareness (Shankweiler & Liberman, 1989). This is a sizable population. Without early preventive measures, many of these children end up being labeled learning disabled or dyslexic and continue to fall behind their peers in reading development (Snider, 1995). They will, by necessity, have to rely on sight-word reading which will quickly become cumbersome and inefficient. In addition, these struggling readers tend to read less, have fewer exposures to words, and are less likely to memorize a large number of these words—further complicating their reading difficulties. However, this doesn't have to be the scenario. Promising phonemic awareness training studies have revealed two important points:

1. phonemic awareness can be taught, and

2. it doesn't take significant amounts of time to bring many children's phonemic awareness abilities up to a level at which phonics instruction will begin to make sense. In fact, some studies have shown results in as few as 11–15 hours of intensive phonemic awareness training spread out over an appropriate time period.

Tips on Sequencing Instruction

- The first four phonemic awareness task types (see pages 4–5) should be a part of the kindergarten curriculum, although all the task types won't be mastered by all children.

- **Rhyming, alliteration,** and **oddity task** activities (with picture clues) are relatively easy for kindergartners.

- **Oral blending** and **oral segmentation** are the two most important phonemic awareness tasks and the focus of many activities in this book.

  —**Oral blending** exercises help children hear how sounds are put together to make words. Oral blending exercises begin with blending larger word parts, such as syllables, and progress to blending onsets and rimes, and finally whole words sound by sound. These activities will lead to decoding, in which children begin sounding out or blending words independently. Children who have difficulty orally blending words will have difficulty blending, or sounding out, words while reading.

  —**Oral segmentation** activities help children separate words into sounds. These exercises should begin with a focus on syllables, which are easier to distinguish than are individual sounds. Segmentation activities will lead to spelling, in which children begin segmenting words into their component sounds in order to write them. Children who have difficulty orally segmenting words will have difficulty breaking apart words in order to spell them.

- **Phonemic manipulation** tasks are more complex. Some of the easier tasks can be mastered by some kindergartners. However, many phonemic manipulation tasks are difficult even for second graders. I recommend the introduction of these tasks *no earlier than middle to late first grade.*

Note that each task type does not have to be mastered before moving on to the next task. A mix of appropriately sequenced activities throughout lessons keeps children engaged and provides ample practice with all types of phonemic awareness tasks. *However, instruction in oral blending should begin before instruction in oral segmentation.*

In addition to these five task types, phonemic

awareness exercises include phoneme discrimination (speech perception) activities which also help children to focus on specific sounds in words. For example, children might be asked to listen for vowel sounds. Since vowel sounds are necessary for decoding, and children's early invented spellings often omit vowels, much practice should be provided to help children hear and distinguish these sounds in words.

Assessment

To determine children's phonemic awareness abilities, give one of the following commercially available assessments:

- **Test of Phonological Awareness,** or **TOPA** (Torgeson and Bryant, 1994). Austin, TX: Pro-Ed.

- **Scholastic Phonemic Awareness Assessment** available in the Scholastic *Phonemic Awareness Kit,* Scholastic, 1997.

- **Yopp-Singer Test of Phonemic Awareness** in "A Test for Assessing Phonemic Awareness in Young Children" (Yopp, 1995), *The Reading Teacher,* 49 (1), pp. 20–29.

If these tests are not available, you can select activities from this book to individually assess each child. Begin assessment in mid-year kindergarten and continue to assess at the beginnings of grades 1–3. Some activities to use:

- Picture Cards, p. 9 (skill: rhyme, oddity task)
- Put It Together, p. 23 (skill: oral blending)
- Count the Sounds, p. 29 (skill: oral segmentation)

How to Use the Book's Poems and Songs

Throughout my years as a teacher, writer, and staff developer, I have collected many poems, songs, and activities ideal for use with phonemic awareness training. I chose the poems and songs in this book based on their:

- popularity with teachers and children,
- musicality and playfulness,
- link to the focused sound, and

- adaptability for use in phonemic awareness activities.

When introducing each poem or song, I suggest the following instructional routine. In addition, I have included two related activities that can be done in the days following the poem or song's initial introduction.

Instructional Routine

1. Play the poem or song on the audio CD for children to enjoy.
2. Distribute photocopies of the poem or song. (Children might enjoy coloring the illustrations.) You may also write the poem or song on chart paper.
3. Read the poem or song aloud as you track the print.
4. Reread it doing one or all of the following:

   - Have children point out the rhyming words. Then frame the rhyming words as you reread. Now have children clap every time you read one of the rhyming words. In later readings, pause before the rhyming words and let children provide them.

   - Substitute poem or song words. For example, using a self-sticking note, substitute the first word in a rhyming pair. Children then suggest a rhyming word to replace the second word in the pair. Write the word on a self-sticking note and place it in the appropriate place in the poem. Help children read the "new" poem or song.

   - Have children clap the rhythm of the poem or song as you read it aloud.

   - Have children substitute the syllable *la* for every syllable they hear in the poem or song.

5. Introduce the accompanying activities.

Enjoy!
—Wiley Blevins

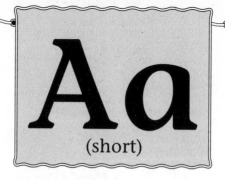

Aa
(short)

Rags

I have a dog and his name is Rags.
He eats so much that his tummy sags.

His ears flip-flop,
And his tail wig-wags,

And when he walks,
He goes zig-zag.

8

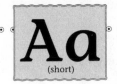

Learning with the Poem

**To focus on the short *a* sound, follow the Instructional Routine on page 7.
Then select one or both of the following activities.**

ACTIVITY 1: Picture Cards
Skill: Rhyme, Oddity Task

Make a set of picture cards (pictures only, no words) using index cards and drawings or magazine pictures. Picture cards are also available on pages 70–71. (*Picture cards are particularly helpful for younger children. The visual cues allow them to think about the sounds in words without having to store a lot of information in their memory.*) Model for children the concept of rhyme using the following model:

Rhyme Model: Model for children how to make a rhyme. For example, you might say "The words *rag* and *wag* rhyme because they sound the same at the end. They both end with /ag/. I can make another word that rhymes with *rag* and *wag*. This word begins with /s/ and ends with /ag/. It's *sag*. Can you make a word that rhymes with *rag* and *wag*?"

Then display a picture card set such as the following: *bat, cat, cake*. Mix the cards, and have children select the two cards whose names rhyme. When two cards are selected, say aloud the name of each picture and ask children to tell you what sounds they have in common. Then have children suggest other words that rhyme with the two picture names. Continue with these picture card sets: *cat, hat, coat; fan, pan, sock; man, can, mop; bat, hat, boat*.

ACTIVITY 2: Do You Know?
Skill: Rhyme

Write the song "Do You Know?" on chart paper. Sing it to the tune of "Muffin Man." Track the print as you sing. Sing the song several times, asking children to suggest one-syllable rhyming words to replace the words *rag* and *wag*. Write the words on self-sticking notes and place them in the appropriate place in the song.

Do You Know?
Do you know two rhyming words,
Two rhyming words,
Two rhyming words?
Oh, do you know two rhyming words?
They sound a lot alike.

<u>Rag</u> and <u>wag</u> are two rhyming words,
Two rhyming words,
Two rhyming words.
<u>Rag</u> and <u>wag</u> are two rhyming words.
They sound a lot alike.

Aa
(long)

Rain
Mother Goose rhyme

Rain, rain, go away,
Come again another day,
Little Johnny wants to play.
Rain, rain, go away.

Phonemic Awareness Songs and Rhymes   Scholastic Professional Books, 1999

 onset - pockogtel

Aa
(long)

Learning with the Poem

To focus on the long *a* sound, follow the Instructional Routine on page 7. Then select one or both of the following activities.

ACTIVITY 1: Blend Baseball
Skill: Oral Blending

On a rainy day when they have indoor recess, engage children in a game of Blend Baseball. Divide the class into two teams. Select the first player on one team. Then say aloud a word in parts, such as /r/...ain. If the child can blend the word, he or she can go to first base. Play the game just like baseball.
You might wish to use the following word parts (*onset and rimes*):

/s/...ay	/r/...ay
/m/...ay	/d/...ay
/l/...ate	/m/...ake
/n/...ail	/r/...ake
/s/...ave	/t/...ame
/w/...ait	/b/...ake

When children become skilled at blending words by onset and rime (/r/...ain), repeat the game asking them to blend words phoneme by phoneme (/r/ /ā/ /n/).

ACTIVITY 2: Who Is It?
Skill: Oral Segmentation, Oral Blending

When lining up for lunch, recess, or a special class such as art, engage children in this guessing game: Say the first sound in a student's name. For example, say /j/. Provide time for children to list all classmates' names that begin with /j/, such as Jane, Johnny, Jamal, and Jessica. Then provide a second clue by providing the next sound in the name. For example, /ā/. Have children guess which classmate you want to line up. After the student's name is correctly identified (Jane), that student can line up and the game continues.

Bb

Betty Botter

Betty Botter bought some butter.
"But," she said, "this butter's bitter.
If I put it in my batter,
It will make my batter bitter.
But a bit of better butter
Would make my batter better."
So it was better Betty Botter
Bought a bit of better butter.

Phonemic Awareness Songs and Rhymes Scholastic Professional Books, 1999

Learning with the Poem

**To focus on the /b/ sound, follow the Instructional Routine on page 7.
Then select one or both of the following activities.**

ACTIVITY 1: Bag Full of B's
Skill: Oddity Task

Place in a bag the following picture cards from pages 70–71: *ball, bat, bee, boat, box, bus, cat, dog, fan, mop, sun*. Mix the cards. Tell children that you want to make a "bag full of B's." To help you, children will find all the picture cards whose names begin with /b/. Have a volunteer select one picture card from the bag and say the picture name. If the picture's name begins with /b/, the child is to place the picture in a pocket chart or on the chalkboard ledge. If the child selects a picture card whose name does not begin with /b/, repeat the picture name extending or reiterating the first sound. Ask, "What sound does this word begin with?" When completed, remind children that all the picture card names in the pocket chart begin with /b/. Then have children suggest other words that begin with /b/. Invite children to make picture cards for these words. Place these picture cards (and those in the pocket chart) back in the bag. Put the bag in a learning center for children to use when reviewing words with /b/. In later days, continue with other sounds and picture card sets.

ACTIVITY 2: Silly Sentences
Skill: Alliteration

Help children to create silly alliterative sentences using words with /b/. For example, "Big bugs bake batches of buttery biscuits." You might wish to begin by helping children generate a list of *b* words on the chalkboard. Create an alliteration book using the sentences and have each child illustrate his or her sentence.

Cc

Birds' Square Dance

by Beverly McLoughland

Swing your partner
Cockatoo
Bluefoot booby
Marabou

Cassowary
Heel and toe
Toucan, noddy
Oriole

Chachalaca
To the right
Bobolink and
Hold her tight

Kittiwake and
Tap your feet
Loon and puffin
Parakeet

Flap your feathers
Curlew, crow
Pipit, tern, and
Do-si-do.

Phonemic Awareness Songs and Rhymes   Scholastic Professional Books, 1999

Learning with the Poem

**To focus on the /k/c sound, follow the Instructional Routine on page 7.
Then select one or both of the following activities.**

ACTIVITY 1: Consonant Riddles
Skill: Phonemic Manipulation

Explain to children that you're going to play a consonant riddle game. You'll say a word. Then they think of a word that rhymes with your word and starts with a given sound. For example:

Teacher: What rhymes with *grow* and starts with /k/?

Children: crow

Continue with these and other riddles:

- What rhymes with *man* and starts with /k/? (*can*)

- What rhymes with *bake* and starts with /k/? (*cake*)

- What rhymes with *goat* and starts with /k/? (*coat*)

- What rhymes with *pup* and starts with /k/? (*cup*)

ACTIVITY 2: Break-the-Code Game
Skill: Oral Blending

Divide the class into teams of 3 to 5 players. Say a word in parts and ask one of the teams to "break the code." For example, if you say the word parts /k/...at, the team should respond with the word *cat*. If that team gets it wrong, give other teams the opportunity to provide the correct answer, modeling how to string together the word parts to say the word as a whole. Teams get one point for each code they break. Play until one team has ten points.

You might wish to use these and other word parts:

/k/...an

/k/...ake

/k/...oat

/k/...ap

/k/...andle

/k/...astle

/k/...offee

/k/...olor

Dd

Dance

by Eve Merriam

Dance out of bed,
dance on the floor,
dance down the hallway,
dance out the door.

Dance in the morning,
dance in the night,
dance till the new moon
is out of sight.

Dance all summer,
autumn and spring,
dance through the snowflakes
and don't forget to sing.

Learning with the Poem

**To focus on the /d/ sound, follow the Instructional Routine on page 7.
Then select one or both of the following activities.**

ACTIVITY 1: Mystery Sentences
Skill: Oral Blending

Read aloud sentences from a book, or sentences that you create. In each sentence choose one word to read in sound segments instead of as a whole word. The children must orally blend the word and then say it. Use sentences in which the children cannot guess the word based on context clues.

Teacher: The little girl danced out of /b/ /e/ /d/. Danced out of what?

Class: bed

Use these and other sentences:

⊙ I saw a big, black /d/ /o/ /g/. What did I see? (a dog)

⊙ The /d/ /u/ /k/ swam in the pond. What swam in the pond? (the duck)

⊙ I put on my /r/ /e/ /d/ dress. What color was my dress? (red)

⊙ The little boy was /s/ /a/ /d/. The little boy was what? (sad)

⊙ The /d/ /i/ /sh/ is dirty. What is dirty? (the dish)

ACTIVITY 2: Team Sound-Off
Skill: Oral Blending

Divide the class into teams of three or four children. Assign each team a sound, such as /d/. Then call three children to the front of the classroom, for example one child from the /b/ group, one child from the /e/ group, and one child from the /d/ group. Have the three children sequence their sounds to form a word. Then they should say the sounds and ask the rest of the class to blend together the sounds to form the word. Teams take turns answering, and each team that guesses correctly gets one point.

Use these sounds and words: /a/, /b/, /d/, /e/, /f/, /h/, /l/, /m/, /p/, /ɾ/, /s/; *bad, bed, fed, had, led, mad, pad, red, sad.*

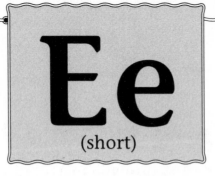

Ee
(short)

Three Little Monkeys

Three little monkeys jumping on the bed,
One fell off and bumped his head.
Jenny called the doctor
And the doctor said,
"No more monkeys jumping on the bed."

Phonemic Awareness Songs and Rhymes Scholastic Professional Books, 1999

Ee
(short)

Learning with the Poem

**To focus on the short *e* sound, follow the Instructional Routine on page 7.
Then select one or both of the following activities.**

ACTIVITY 1: Listening Center
Skill: Oral Segmentation

Place a tape recorder and a set of blocks in a listening center. On a tape, read aloud a list of ten words. Have children number a piece of paper from 1 to 10. Then, as they hear each word read, have them move one block for each sound they hear in the word. Have them count the number of blocks (the number of sounds in the word) and record that number on their paper. Provide the answers at the end of the tape for children to self-correct their papers. (You might wish to begin the tape by modeling a sample. For example, *"bed* has three sounds—/b/ /e/ /d/." Use the following ten words:

1. leg (/l/ /e/ /g/)
2. egg (/e/ /g/)
3. sell (/s/ /e/ /l/)
4. ten (/t/ /e/ /n/)
5. Ed (/e/ /d/)
6. led (/l/ /e/ /d/)
7. sled (/s/ /l/ /e/ /d/)
8. vet (/v/ /e/ /t/)
9. desk (/d/ /e/ /s/ /k/)
10. check (/ch/ /e/ /k/)

ACTIVITY 2: Roll Call
Skill: Oral Segmentation

When taking attendance, say each child's name without the beginning sound. For example, you would say "enny" for Jenny. When a volunteer identifies the correct student, have the class provide the missing sound (/j/). During later weeks, have volunteers assume the role of "teacher" and take roll call in this way.

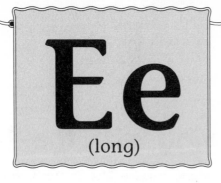

Ee
(long)

I Eat My Peas with Honey
by Gellette Burgess

I eat my peas with honey.
I've done it all my life.
It makes the peas taste funny,
But it keeps them on the knife.

Phonemic Awareness Songs and Rhymes   Scholastic Professional Books, 1999

Ee
(long)

Learning with the Poem

**To focus on the long *e* sound, follow the Instructional Routine on page 7.
Then select one or both of the following activities.**

ACTIVITY 1: Secret Sound
Skill: Oral Segmentation

Explain to children that you're going to play a word game. You'll say three words, and you want them to listen closely and tell you what sound they hear that is the same in all the words. For example, if you say *meet, bean,* and *teeth,* children should respond with /ē/. Make sure the target sound is in the same position (initial, medial, or final) in all the words. Continue with these and other word sets:

- feet, mean, team
- deep, feed, neat
- life, knife, kite
- peas, pan, pail
- top, map, lip
- meat, seed, leaf
- bed, had, hid
- make, bike, joke
- sit, soap, safe

ACTIVITY 2: Push the Pea
Skill: Oral Segmentation

Have children draw four connected boxes on a sheet of paper. (See sample below.) Then distribute to each child four dried peas, beans, or other food markers. Say one word at a time. Have children push one pea into each box for each sound they hear in the word. For example, if you say the word *peas,* children should push one dried pea into each of three boxes (/p/ /ē/ /z/). Continue with other words such as *me, team, see, seed, keep, eat, leap, sleep.* This activity can also be placed in a learning center. Instead of stating a word, provide a set of picture cards. Use these and other picture cards from pages 70–71: *bee* (2), *feet* (3), *leaf* (3), *tie* (2), *fish* (3), *nest* (4), *sock* (3), *snake* (4), *kite* (3). To make the activity self-checking, write the number of sounds each picture name contains on the back of the card.

Ff

Five Little Fishies

Five little fishies swimming in a pool.
First one said, "The pool is cool."
Second one said, "The pool is deep."
Third one said, "I want to sleep."
Fourth one said, "Let's dive and dip."
Fifth one said, "I spy a ship."
Fisherman's boat comes,
Line goes ker-splash,
Away the five little fishies dash.

Phonemic Awareness Songs and Rhymes   Scholastic Professional Books, 1999

Learning with the Poem

To focus on the /f/ sound, follow the Instructional Routine on page 7.
Then select one or both of the following activities.

ACTIVITY 1: Put It Together
Skill: Oral Blending

Make a sock puppet in the form of a fish. Tell children that for this activity you will say a word in parts. They should listen carefully and orally blend the parts to say the word as a whole. For example, if you say /f/ /i/ /n/, they are to respond with *fin*.

> *Oral Blending Model:* Model for children how to blend sounds into words. For example, you might say "I'm going to say a word very slowly, sound by sound. Then, I'll say the word a bit faster. Finally, I'll say the word the way it is usually said. For example, if I hear the word parts /f/ /i/ /n/, I can blend them together like this: *ffffiiiinnnn, ffiinn, fin.*"

Begin the modeling of blending with short CVC words (i.e., *sat*, *sun*, *map*) that start with continuous consonants such as *m, s, l, f,* and *r*. To help children visually note when you change from sound to sound as you blend the word, add movements. For example, you might move your hands from right to left as you change from sound to sound. You might also want to point out the mouth position (lips, tongue) and throat vibration (if applicable) when making each sound. Then use these words for blending practice:

- ⊙ fish
- ⊙ fan
- ⊙ fun
- ⊙ fit
- ⊙ feed
- ⊙ five

ACTIVITY 2: Initial Sound Switch
Skill: Phonemic Manipulation

Explain to children that you're going to play a word game. They're going to make new words by replacing the first sound in each word you say with /f/. For example, if you say the word *dish*, children are to say *fish*. Continue with these and other words: *dive, door, ran, sun, sit, box, cat.*

Extension: After children become skilled at substituting initial consonant sounds, have them substitute final consonant sounds (i.e., replace the last sound in *man* with /p/—*map*) and then medial vowel sounds (i.e., replace the middle sound in *ride* with /ō/—*rode*). Do not begin these exercises until mid-year grade one or later.

Gg

Gobble, Gobble

A turkey is a funny bird,
His head goes wobble, wobble,
And he knows just one word,
Gobble, gobble, gobble.

Phonemic Awareness Songs and Rhymes   Scholastic Professional Books, 1999

Gg

Learning with the Poem

**To focus on the /g/ sound, follow the Instructional Routine on page 7.
Then select one or both of the following activities.**

ACTIVITY 1: Sound Search
Skill: Phonemic Manipulation

Say a three-phoneme word and the sound you are searching for. For example, say *gobble* and ask for the first sound (/g/), or *gate* and ask for the middle sound (/ā/). Use the following words and "Sound Search" questions:

- *bag*:
  What's the ending sound? (/g/)
- *goat*:
  What's the beginning sound? (/g/)
- *leaf*:
  What's the middle sound? (/ē/)
- *sell*:
  What's the beginning sound? (/s/)
- *leg*:
  What's the ending sound? (/g/)
- *game*:
  What's the middle sound? (/ā/)
- *go*:
  What's the beginning sound? (/g/)
- *top*:
  What's the ending sound? (/p/)

ACTIVITY 2: Turkey Talk
Skill: Oral Blending

If available, display a picture of a turkey. Explain to children that this turkey has problems gobbling. Instead of speaking quickly, it can only say words very slowly. Children are to help the turkey by saying the word at its natural pace. Then, say a word very slowly—stretching each sound. For example, you might say *lllleeeeg*. Have children repeat the stretched out word. Then have them say the word correctly. To provide children with help, slowly compress the word—*lllleeeeg, lleeg, leg*. Continue with these and other words: *log, rag, rug, fig*.

Hh

Hillary Hume

Hillary Hume has a hundred hamsters.
A hundred hamsters has Hillary Hume.
If Hillary Hume has a hundred hamsters,
Will you share a room with Hillary Hume?

Phonemic Awareness Songs and Rhymes   Scholastic Professional Books, 1999

Learning with the Poem

To focus on the /h/ sound, follow the Instructional Routine on page 7.
Then select one or both of the following activities.

ACTIVITY 1:
Billary-Hillary Ball Game
Skill: Phonemic Manipulation, Rhyme

Have children sit in a circle on the floor. Explain to them that you are going to say a word. Then you will roll a ball to someone in the circle. That person must say a word that rhymes with your word and begins with /h/. For example, if you say *candle*, the person you roll the ball to must say *handle*. Use these and other words: *cat, ram, card, pair, tall, sand, late, may, part, seat, sigh, will, Jim, sip, sit, five, mole, good, took, mop, rope, mouse, got.*

ACTIVITY 2: Syllable Drop
Skill: Syllables

Have children place their fingers under their chins. Then say aloud a word syllable by syllable. Explain to children that when you say each syllable, or word part, your chin drops. Have children repeat the word and count the number of syllables (chin drops) in each word. Continue by stating aloud a word and asking children to say it syllable by syllable, counting the number of syllables (chin drops) they hear (feel). Use these and other words: *hamster* (2), *hundred* (2), *Hillary* (3), *had* (1), *hamburger* (3), *handle* (2), *happy* (2).

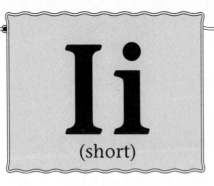

Ii
(short)

This Little Pig Went to Market

Mother Goose rhyme

This little pig went to market;
This little pig stayed at home;
This little pig had roast beef;
This little pig had none;
And this little pig cried, Wee-wee-wee,
And ran all the way home.

Phonemic Awareness Songs and Rhymes Scholastic Professional Books, 1999

Learning with the Poem

To focus on the short *i* sound, follow the Instructional Routine on page 7. Then select one or both of the following activities.

ACTIVITY 1: Quick Draw
Skill: Oral Blending, Oral Segmentation

Place in a bag the following picture cards from pages 70–71: *pig, fish, six*. Draw out one card at a time, not showing it to children. Tell children that you see, for example, a /p/…ig. Ask them to orally blend the word parts to guess the picture name. Display the card so children can check their responses. Then invite children to be the "teacher" and segment the words for the class to guess. When children become skilled at segmenting and blending words by onset and rime (/p/…ig), repeat the activity, asking them to segment and blend the words phoneme by phoneme (/p/ /i/ /g/).

ACTIVITY 2: Count the Sounds
Skill: Oral Segmentation

Distribute five counters to each child. Then have children draw a series of three connected boxes on a sheet of paper (see sample below).

Explain that you're going to read aloud a word. Tell them that they should count how many sounds they hear in the word and place one counter on a box on their paper for each sound they hear. For example, if you say the word *sit*, children should place three counters on their paper, one on each box. You may need to extend the sounds in each word to be sure children hear each discrete sound. For example, you may need to say *ssssiiiit* for children having difficulty distinguishing the sounds in the word *sit*. And you may want to add movements. For example, move your hands from right to left as you say the word, emphasizing when you change from one sound to another.

Have children segment each of the three related words in each column listed below before moving on to the next column. Help them understand that only one sound is different in each new word in the column. Ask them which sound in each new word is different.

Use these and other words:

it	at	mop	run	in	cup
sit	sat	map	sun	pin	cap
fit	sit	tap	bun	pan	cat

Variation to the segmentation boxes: Have children do one of the following:

- Slap their knee the number of sounds they hear.

- Walk in place or march the number of sounds they hear in a word.

- Play on a musical instrument one note for each sound they hear. For example, beat on the drum one time for each sound in a word.

29

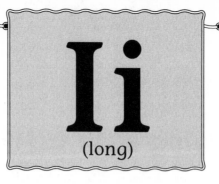

Ii
(long)

Three Blind Mice

Mother Goose rhyme

Three blind mice, see how they run!
They all ran after the farmer's wife,
Who cut off their tails with a carving knife,
Did you ever see such a thing in your life,
    As three blind mice?

Phonemic Awareness Songs and Rhymes Scholastic Professional Books, 1999

Learning with the Poem

**To focus on the long *i* sound, follow the Instructional Routine on page 7.
Then select one or both of the following activities.**

ACTIVITY 1: Every Word Counts
Skill: Concept of "word"

Write each word of the first line of "Three Blind Mice" on individual index cards. Assign one card to each of seven children. Have the children stand in front of the classroom in sentence order. Ask the class to count the number of words in the sentence. Then ask children to say the word on their card as you point to them in correct order. To emphasize the importance of word order, point to each child in reverse order as they say the rhyme backwards. You might also wish to mix the order, have children say the mixed-up sentence, then ask the rest of the class to fix it. Continue with additional lines in this or other poems.

ACTIVITY 2: Animal Rhymes
Skill: Rhyme

Write the following incomplete rhymes on the chalkboard or on chart paper. Tell children that they must name a word that rhymes with the underlined word to finish each rhyme.

- Some <u>mice</u> eating _____.
- A <u>fly</u> zooming up in the _____.
- A <u>mouse</u> living in a _____.
- A <u>goat</u> sailing on a _____.
- A <u>cat</u> wearing a big, red _____.
- A <u>dog</u> sitting on a _____.
- A <u>bug</u> hiding under a _____.
- A <u>duck</u> driving a _____.
- A <u>moose</u> chasing after a _____.
- A <u>pig</u> wearing a silly _____.

Jj

Jack

Mother Goose rhyme

Jack be nimble,
Jack be quick,
Jack jump over
The candlestick.

Phonemic Awareness Songs and Rhymes   Scholastic Professional Books, 1999

Learning with the Poem

To focus on the /j/ sound, follow the Instructional Routine on page 7.
Then select one or both of the following activities.

ACTIVITY 1: Alphabet Actions
Skill: Sound Discrimination

When introducing /j/ or any other sound, assign a movement whose name begins with the sound. For example, tell children that they will "jump" every time you say /j/ or a word that begins with /j/. Then read aloud a list of words such as the following: *jar, jelly, sand, jeep, goat, leaf, jam, jet, jiggle*. When working with other sounds, you might wish to use the following movements (from *Phonics They Use: Words for Reading and Writing,* Patricia Cunningham, HarperCollins, 1995):

b: bounce	n: nod
c: catch	p: paint
d: dance	r: run
f: fall	s: sit
g: gallop	t: talk
h: hop	v: vacuum
j: jump	w: walk
k: kick	y: yawn
l: laugh	z: zip
m: march	

* You can use these same movements when teaching sound-spelling relationships during phonics lessons (for example, the letter *j* stands for /j/ as in *jump*).

ACTIVITY 2: Row Your Boat
Skill: Phonemic Manipulation

Write the song "Row Your Boat" on chart paper. Have children sing the song a few times. Then tell them that you'll sing it again, but this time you'll change the line "Merrily, merrily, merrily, merrily," to "Jerrily, jerrily, jerrily, jerrily." To illustrate this, write the word *merrily* on the chalkboard, erase the letter *m*, and replace it with the letter *j*. Pronounce the nonsense word formed. This will show children that replacing one sound in a word creates a new word. Continue singing the song. Each time, change the first letter in the word *merrily* to create a new third line. You might choose to use the nonsense words *serrily, werrily,* and *berrily*.

Row Your Boat
Row, row, row your boat,
Gently down the stream.
Merrily, merrily, merrily, merrily,
Life is but a dream.

Kk

100 Is a Lot!
by Meish Goldish

100 dogs, 100 cats,
100 heads for 100 hats.
100 women, 100 men,
100's more than 5 or 10.
100 buttons, 100 coats,
100 sails for 100 boats.
100 cookies, 100 cakes,
100 kids with bellyaches!
100 shoes, 100 socks,
100 keys for 100 locks.
100 puddles mighty dirty,
100's even more than 30.
100 daughters, 100 sons,
100 franks, 100 buns.
100 trees, 100 plants,
100 picnics, 100 ants!
100 is a lot to count,
100 is a LARGE AMOUNT!
100 kisses, 100 hugs,
100 bats and 100 bugs.
100 bees, 100 birds,
This poem has 100 words!

34

Phonemic Awareness Songs and Rhymes Scholastic Professional Books, 1999

Learning with the Poem

To focus on the /k/ sound, follow the Instructional Routine on page 7.
Then select one or both of the following activities.

ACTIVITY 1: Picture Rhyme
Skill: Rhyme

Have children fold a piece of paper in half. Ask them to draw pictures of two things whose names rhyme. For example, a *sock* and a *lock*. Suggest that children choose objects whose names begin or end with /k/. Help children label the pictures with the items' names. Gather the drawings and bind them into a rhyme book for the class library.

TIP: Provide children who are struggling with this activity with the name of one item from the poem to draw, such as a *key, cake, hat, boat, plant, bug,* or *bun.* Then have them come up with the second item.

ACTIVITY 2: Draw It
Skill: Oral Blending

Have each child fold a sheet of paper into fourths. Then orally segment the name of an easily drawn object, such as a *cake.* Use this and other words from "100 Is a Lot!" Ask children to orally blend the word parts and then draw a picture of the word in one section of their paper. In the early exercises, segment the words by onset and rime, such as /k/...ake. In later exercises, segment the words phoneme by phoneme, such as /k/ /ā/ /k/. Begin with two- or three-phoneme names (e.g., key—/k/ /ē/; cat—/k/ /a/ /t/) and progress to four-phoneme names (e.g., box—/b/ /o/ /k/ /s/; socks—/s/ /o/ /k/ /s/).

Ll

Looby Loo

Here we go looby loo,
Here we go looby light.
Here we go looby loo
All on a Saturday night.

Put your right hand in,
Put your right hand out,
Shake it a little, a little,
And turn yourself about.

We've included additional verses on the audio CD.

Phonemic Awareness Songs and Rhymes   Scholastic Professional Books, 1999

Learning with the Song

**To focus on the /l/ sound, follow the Instructional Routine on page 7.
Then select one or both of the following activities.**

ACTIVITY 1: Sound of the Day
Skill: Phonemic Manipulation

Select a sound of the day, such as /l/. Throughout the day, say children's names with the first sound replaced by the sound of the day. Peter would be called "Leter," Bonnie would be called "Lonnie," and Harry would be called "Larry." You may want to take attendance this way and you may want to encourage each child to experiment with saying his or her classmates' names with the sound of the day.

ACTIVITY 2: Seeing Sounds
Skill: Speech Perception

To help children understand that different sounds are made in different ways, choose two contrasting sounds such as /l/ and /f/. Then distribute small mirrors to each child. If mirrors are unavailable, have children face a partner for this activity. Then say the first sound (/l/) and have children repeat it as they look in the mirror or at their partner. Ask children what position their tongue and lips are in when making this sound. Suggest that they watch your mouth as you make the sound. Then have them feel whether or not a burst of air is made with the sound by placing their hand in front of their mouths as they say the sound. Continue by having them place their hand on their throat to feel if a vibration occurs when making the sound.

When completed, have them say and observe the production of the contrasting sound /f/. Compare and discuss the way each sound is made. Continue with other highly contrasting sounds such as /k/-/m/; /s/-/p/; /j/-/t/; and /w/-/d/.

Mm

Old MacDonald Had a Farm

Old MacDonald had a farm, E-I-E-I-O.
And on that farm he had a cow, E-I-E-I-O.
With a moo, moo here
And a moo, moo there,
Here a moo, there a moo,
Everywhere a moo, moo.
Old MacDonald had a farm, E-I-E-I-O.

We've included additional verses on the audio CD.

Phonemic Awareness Songs and Rhymes   Scholastic Professional Books, 1999

Learning with the Song

**To focus on the /m/ sound, follow the Instructional Routine on page 7.
Then select one or both of the following activities.**

Activity 1:
Old MacDonald Had a Box
Skill: Oral Blending

Write the song "Old MacDonald Had a Box" on chart paper. Explain to children that this is a different version of the song "Old MacDonald Had a Farm." Sing the song several times. During each singing, introduce different items that could be in Old MacDonald's box by orally segmenting a different one-syllable word for children to blend. Select words that begin with /m/. You might segment each word by onset and rime (/m/...ap) or phoneme by phoneme (/m/ /a/ /p/) depending on children's instructional level. Use the following word parts: /m/...ouse, /m/...ask, /m/ /o/ /p/, /m/ /a/ /t/, /m/ /u/ /g/.

Old MacDonald Had a Box

Old MacDonald had a box, E-I-E-I-O.
And in that box he had a /m/...ap, E-I-E-I-O
With a <u>map</u>, <u>map</u> here
And a <u>map</u>, <u>map</u> there,
Here a <u>map</u>, there a <u>map</u>,
Everywhere a <u>map</u>, <u>map</u>.
Old MacDonald had a box, E-I-E-I-O.

Activity 2: Where Is It?
Skill: Oral Segmentation

This activity helps children differentiate sound position in words. Distribute one counter to each child. Then have children each draw three connected boxes on a sheet of paper (see sample below). Explain that you're going to say a list of words that all contain /m/. Some words contain /m/ at the beginning, some in the middle, and some at the end. Tell children that if they hear /m/ at the beginning of the word, they should place the counter in the first box. If they hear /m/ in the middle, they should place their counter in the center box. And if they hear /m/ at the end, they should place their counter in the last box. You'll be able to check quickly for accuracy. You may wish to use the following word list: *man, moon, ham, summer, room, hammer, made, dream, lemon.*

In subsequent days, continue with other sounds and word lists such as the following:

/s/—send, missing, sock, bus, less, passing, messy, safe

/p/—pack, mop, happy, pocket, hope, open, trap, pencil, keep

/d/—dog, duck, pad, pudding, middle, door, toad, read, puddle, dig

Nn

Engine, Engine, Number Nine

Engine, Engine, Number Nine,
Running on the Chicago line.
See it sparkle, see it shine,
Engine, Engine, Number Nine.

Phonemic Awareness Songs and Rhymes   Scholastic Professional Books, 1999

Nn

Learning with the Poem

**To focus on the /n/ sound, follow the Instructional Routine on page 7.
Then select one or both of the following activities.**

ACTIVITY 1: All Aboard!
Skill: Alliteration

Invite children to sit in a circle. Tell them that you're going on an imaginary trip on Engine, Engine, Number Nine. Explain that you will tell them one item that you want to take on the trip. They are to take turns repeating that item name, and then name another item whose name begins with the same sound. Start with items whose names begin with /n/. For example, if you say, "I'm going on Engine, Engine, Number Nine and I'm taking a *nail*," the next child in the circle might say, "I'm going on Engine, Engine, Number Nine and I'm taking a *nail* and a *notebook*." Continue around the circle until children run out of items whose names begin with /n/.

ACTIVITY 2: Train Car Load Up
Skill: Oral Segmentation

Clean out some old milk cartons and have children cut off the tops and decorate three cartons to look like train cars. Then distribute a handful of raisins to each child. Tell children that the train must be loaded and readied for departure—*Toot! Toot!* To load the train cars, you will say a list of words. All the words contain the /n/ sound. Tell children that if they hear /n/ at the beginning of the word, they should place the raisin in the first car. If they hear /n/ in the middle, they should place their raisin in the center car. And if they hear /n/ at the end, they should place their raisin in the last car. At the end of the activity, allow children to eat their raisins. Use these and other words: *nail, name, lemon, nurse, runner, nickel, seven, dinner, rain, fun, neck.*

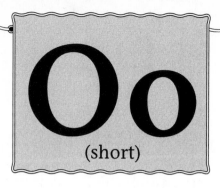

Oo
(short)

Higglety, Pigglety, Pop

Mother Goose rhyme

Higglety, pigglety, pop!
The dog has eaten the mop.
The pig's in a hurry,
The cat's in a flurry,
Higglety, pigglety, pop!

Phonemic Awareness Songs and Rhymes   Scholastic Professional Books, 1999

O o
(short)

Learning with the Poem

**To focus on the short _o_ sound, follow the Instructional Routine on page 7.
Then select one or both of the following activities.**

ACTIVITY 1: Guess It!
Skill: Oral Blending

Guess It! can be played in many ways. In this version, you orally segment the name of an animal. Children guess the animal's identity. Begin with animal names from "Higglety, Pigglety, Pop." For example, you might start by saying:

 I'm thinking of an animal. It's a /d/...og.
   What am I thinking of?

Children: A dog!

Continue with _cat, pig, duck,_ and _fox._ In subsequent days, repeat the activity using words with /o/ such as _mop, pop, box, dot, fog, sock, top, not, mom, lock, jog, hop, hot,_ and _lock._

ACTIVITY 2: Graph It
Skill: Oral Segmentation

Display the following picture cards from pages 70–71: _mop, dog, pig, cat, bee, tie, glass, nest._ Have children sort the cards according to the number of sounds each picture name contains. Then create a graph using the cards.

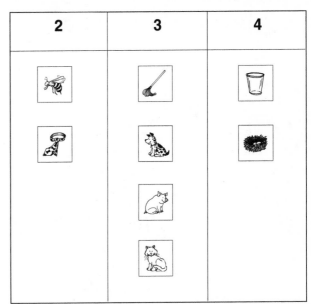

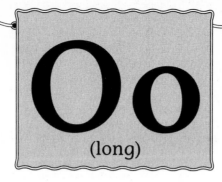

Oo
(long)

Rima de chocolate
traditional Spanish rhyme

Uno, dos, tres, cho-
Uno, dos, tres, -co-
Uno, dos, tres, -la-
Uno, dos, tres, -te
Bate, Bate el chocolate.

Chocolate Rhyme

One, two, three, cho-
One, two, three, -co-
One, two, three, -la-
One, two, three, -te
Stir, stir the chocolate.

Phonemic Awareness Songs and Rhymes Scholastic Professional Books, 1999

Learning with the Poem

To focus on the long *o* sound, follow the Instructional Routine on page 7.
Then select one or both of the following activities.

ACTIVITY 1: S-t-r-e-t-c-h It!
Skill: Oral Blending

Bubble gum, like chocolate, is a favorite childhood treat. Explain to children that they are going to stretch out words in the same way as you stretch out bubble gum. Say a word very slowly, such as *sssssoooo* (so). As you say the word, put your hand to your mouth and pretend to stretch the word as if you are stretching a piece of bubble gum. Then have children repeat and stretch the word. Compress the word by stretching it less and less until you say the word at a natural pace. Have children do the same. Continue the activity with the following words: *soap, roll, nose, note, rope, robe, vote, foam, loaf, moan, road, soak, flow, row, show, snow*. In subsequent days, invite volunteers to suggest words to stretch.

ACTIVITY 2: Can You Say?
Skill: Oral Segmentation

Write the song "Can You Say?" on chart paper. Sing the song to the tune of "Happy Birthday." Track the print as you sing. Sing the song several times. Each time, replace the word *yellow* with one of the following words: *shadow, window, swallow, pillow, mitten, happen, tablet, rabbit*. Pause to provide children time to isolate the ending sound in each word. It might be necessary to emphasize the ending sound of each word for children having difficulties.

Can You Say?
Can you say the last sound?
Can you say the last sound?
It's the last sound in <u>yellow</u>.
Can you say the last sound?

45

Pp

Pin Pón

traditional Mexican song

Pin Pón es un muñeco
De trapo y de cartón,
Se lava su carita
Con agua y con jabón.

Se desenreda el pelo
Con peine de marfil,
Y aunque se dé estirones,
No llora ni hace así.

Pin Pón

Pin Pón's a paper doll
And his clothes are all in place,
He uses soap and water
To wash his hands and face.

He straightens out his hair
With a tiny ivory comb,
And even if he pulls hard,
He doesn't cry or moan.

Phonemic Awareness Songs and Rhymes   Scholastic Professional Books, 1999

Learning with the Song

To focus on the /p/ sound, follow the Instructional Routine on page 7. Then select one or both of the following activities.

ACTIVITY 1: Picky Paper Puppet
Skill: Oddity Task

Distribute a set of picture cards (see pages 70–71) evenly among the children. Each child should have at least two cards. Then, using a puppet made of paper, explain to children that this puppet is a "sound puppet" who likes only things whose names begin with a sound it chooses. For example, if the puppet likes potatoes, it will also like other things whose names begin with the /p/ sound. Tell children that the sound puppet will name an object it likes. If they have any picture cards whose names also begin with the first sound in the object's name, they should hold up those cards. Have the puppet provide corrective feedback by reiterating or extending the beginning sound of each card to check children's responses. For example:

Puppet: I like potatoes.

One child holds up the pig *picture card.*

Puppet: I see a pig. P-p-p-pig. *Pig* begins with /p/, just like *potatoes.*

ACTIVITY 2: First Sound First
Skill: Oral Segmentation

Ask children to listen to the following set of words: *pig, pan, pot*. Point out that all these words start with the same sound. This sound is /p/. Tell them that you want them to listen carefully to each new set of words you say and then tell you what the first sound is. Finally ask them to volunteer other words that begin with that sound.

Example: "Can you tell what the first sound is in *pig, pan, pot*? That's right, it's /p/. What other words do you know that begin with /p/?"

Use these and other word sets:
- pack, pen, puddle
- map, mess, mail
- send, sick, sail
- pickle, pop, pit
- keep, kick, key
- leaf, lion, late
- pie, pillow, peach
- fish, fan, fox

Extension: Have children listen for the last sound.

Example: "Can you tell me what the last sound is in *map, top, lip*? That's right, it's /p/. What other words do you know that end with /p/?"

Six Little Ducks

by Marie Winn and Allan Miller

Six little ducks
That I once knew,
Fat ones,
skinny ones,
fair ones too.
But the one little duck
With the feather on his back,
He led the others
With his quack quack quack.

Quack quack quack,
Quack quack quack,
He led the others
With his quack quack quack!

We've included additional verses on the audio CD.

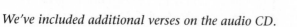

Qq

Learning with the Poem

**To focus on the /kw/ *qu* sounds, follow the Instructional Routine on page 7.
Then select one or both of the following activities.**

ACTIVITY 1: Rhyme Charades
Skill: Rhyme

Ask volunteers to act out rhyming words. State aloud a word, such as *back*. Then have a volunteer act out a rhyming word for the class to guess, such as *quack*. The student who correctly guesses the rhyming word gets to be the person who acts out the next rhyme. Continue until all children have had an opportunity to play charades.

ACTIVITY 2: Rhyme Collage
Skill: Rhyme

Ask children to cut out magazine pictures of objects or actions whose names rhyme, such as *queen* and *bean*, *duck* and *truck*, or *quack* and *track*. Have them make rhyme collages with the pictures. Display the collages on a classroom bulletin board. As a variation, have children cut out magazine pictures of objects whose names begin or end with the same sound. Have them make sound collages with the pictures.

Rr

Jump-Rope Rhymes

1

Jump rope, jump rope,
Will I miss?
Jump rope, jump rope,
Just watch this!

2

Rooms for rent
Inquire within.
As I move out
Let <u>Ronnie</u> come in.

3

Cinderella dressed in red
Went downstairs to bake some bread
How many loaves did she bake?
One, two, three, four, five...

4

Not last night but the night before,
24 robbers came knocking at my door.
As I ran out, they ran in.
I hit them on the head with a rolling pin.

Phonemic Awareness Songs and Rhymes   Scholastic Professional Books, 1999

Learning with the Poems

To focus on the /r/ sound, follow the Instructional Routine on page 7.
Then select one or both of the following activities.

ACTIVITY 1: Jump and Clap
Skill: Oddity Task, Oral Segmentation

Distribute a set of picture cards. (See pages 70–71.) Tell children that you will say a sound. If their picture card's name begins with that sound they are to jump and clap, stand, sit, turn around, or some other designated movement. For example, if you say /f/, the children holding the fan, feet, fish, and frog picture cards should jump and clap. Continue with other sounds.

Once they are familiar with the exercise, tell children that you will say a word. If the word begins with /r/, they are to jump and clap. Use these and other words: *red, rope, dog, tape, run, raisin, deer, roll, cow, cheese, race, rake, road, rub.*

ACTIVITY 2: Construction Time
Skill: Oral Segmentation, Oral Blending

Distribute a set of linking cubes (Unifix cubes, for example) to each child. Tell children that you will say a word. They are to take one cube for each sound they hear and link them together to form a chain representing the number of sounds in the word. For example, children will link together three cubes for the word *red* (/r/ /e/ /d/). When completed, have children break apart the linked chain by pulling off one cube at a time as they say each sound in the word. Use these and other words: *run, ran, rope, rent, roll, row, race, ray, rake, rock, rip, rat, rest, raft.*

Ss

Sing!
by Joe Raposo

Sing.
Sing a song.
Sing out loud.
Sing out strong.

Sing of good things,
Not bad.
Sing of happy,
Not sad.

Sing.
Sing a song.
Make it simple
To last your whole life long.

Don't worry that it's not good enough
For anyone else to hear.
Sing.
Sing a song.

La lalalala…

Learning with the Song

To focus on the /s/ sound, follow the Instructional Routine on page 7. Then select one or both of the following activities.

ACTIVITY 1: Sing to Your Partner
Skill: Oral Segmentation

Distribute a set of picture cards from pages 70–71 to each pair of partners. Have them spread the cards faceup on the table or floor. Then select one person in each pair or group to be the "caller." That person must sing the first sound in one of the picture card names. The partner must then find the correct picture card. If correct, that person becomes the caller. The game continues until all the cards have been selected.

ACTIVITY 2: What's the Sound?
Skill: Oral Segmentation

Write the song "What's the Sound?" on chart paper. Sing it to the tune of "Old MacDonald Had a Farm." Track the print as you sing. Sing the song several times, encouraging children to join in. During later singings, replace the words *sing* and *silly* with the following:

- *mop* and *money*
- *leaf* and *lucky*
- *ten* and *table*

What's the Sound?
What's the sound that these words share?
Listen to these words.
<u>Sing</u> and <u>silly</u> are these two words.
Tell me what you've heard. (*sssssss*)
With a /s/, /s/ here, and a /s/, /s/ there,
Here a /s/, there a /s/, everywhere a /s/, /s/.
/s/ is the sound that these words share.
We can hear that sound!

Tt

Teddy Bear

Teddy Bear, Teddy Bear,
Turn around.
Teddy Bear, Teddy Bear,
Touch the ground.
Teddy Bear, Teddy Bear,
Show your shoe.
Teddy Bear, Teddy Bear,
That will do!

Learning with the Poem

**To focus on the /t/ sound, follow the Instructional Routine on page 7.
Then select one or both of the following activities.**

ACTIVITY 1: Pocket Chart Sort
Skill: Oddity Task

Place in a pocket chart the following picture cards from pages 70–71: *bat, boat, cat, coat, feet, gate, goat, kite, nest, ten, tie, top.* Then on one index card, write t_____. On another write _____t. Have children place picture cards whose names begin with /t/ under t_____, and the cards whose names end with /t/ under _____t. Continue with other cards and sounds.

ACTIVITY 2: One Potato, One Tomato
Skill: Oral Segmentation

Teach the children the rhyme "One Potato." Then have small groups of children sit in a circle. As you say the rhyme, pass around an object such as a small beanbag. The child holding the beanbag at the end of the rhyme (on "more") must then state a word that begins with /p/, the first sound in *potato.* Then repeat the rhyme replacing the word *potato* with the suggested word. Continue until all children have had a chance to suggest a word. Next, change the word *potato* to *tomato.* In this version, the children will state words that begin with /t/. In subsequent days, choose other food names and sounds, such as *zucchini* (/z/) or *banana* (/b/).

> **One Potato**
> One potato, two potato
> Three potato, four,
> Five potato, six potato,
> Seven potato, more.

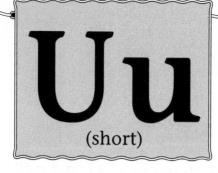

(short)

Wheels on the Bus

The wheels on the bus go 'round and 'round,
'round and 'round,
'round and 'round.
The wheels on the bus go 'round and 'round
All over town.

The wipers on the bus go swish, swish, swish,
swish, swish, swish,
swish, swish, swish.
The wipers on the bus go swish, swish, swish
All over town.

The driver on the bus goes "move on back,
move on back, move on back."
The driver on the bus goes "move on back
All over town."

The people on the bus go up and down,
up and down,
up and down.
The people on the bus go up and down
All over town.

We've included additional verses on the audio CD.

Phonemic Awareness Songs and Rhymes   Scholastic Professional Books, 1999

Learning with the Song

**To focus on the short *u* sound, follow the Instructional Routine on page 7.
Then select one or both of the following activities.**

ACTIVITY 1: Segmentation Cheer
Skill: Oral Segmentation

Write "Segmentation Cheer" on chart paper
and teach children the cheer. Each time you
say the cheer, change the words in the third
line. Have children segment this word sound
by sound. You might want to use these words
in subsequent cheers: *sun, rug, duck, bug, cup,
fun, luck, nut, run.*

Segmentation Cheer
Listen to my cheer.
Then shout the sounds you hear.
Bus! Bus! Bus!
Let's take apart the word *bus*!

Give me the beginning sound.
   (Children respond with /b/.)
Give me the middle sound.
   (Children respond with /u/.)
Give me the ending sound.
   (Children respond with /s/.)

That's right!
/b/ /u/ /s/—Bus! Bus! Bus!

ACTIVITY 2:
The Sounds in the Word
Skill: Oral Blending

Have children sing the following song to the
tune of "The Wheels on the Bus." During
each singing, segment a three-phoneme word
such as *sun, rug, duck, bug, cup, fun, luck, nut,
run.* Children are to orally blend the sounds
and say the whole word when the song is
completed.

The Sounds in the Word
The sounds in the word are /s/ /u/ /n/;
   /s/ /u/ /n/; /s/ /u/ /n/.
The sounds in the word are /s/ /u/ /n/,
Shout the word out loud!

Uu
(long)

Wonderful World
by Eva Grant

I can see
Trees and grass,
The sun and sky;

I can taste
Chocolate ice cream,
Apple pie;

I can hear
Music, laughter,
Words you said;

I can smell
Perfume, flowers,
Baking bread;

I can touch
Silk and velvet,
Baby's skin;

What a wonderful
World I'm in!

Phonemic Awareness Songs and Rhymes Scholastic Professional Books, 1999

Uu
(long)

Learning with the Poem

**To focus on the long _u_ sound, follow the Instructional Routine on page 7.
Then select one or both of the following activities.**

ACTIVITY 1: My World—I Spy
Skill: Oral Segmentation, Oral Blending

Display a favorite picture in a trade book, or have children look around the classroom. Explain to children that you are going to play a game called I Spy. To play, you will say something like "I spy with my little eye something that starts with /yoo/." You want them to guess the name of the object that begins with that sound or sounds. If necessary, provide additional clues such as "It is in a picture on the wall. It is something a police officer wears." (uniform) You might also wish to orally segment an object you see and have children blend the sounds to figure out the object's name. For example, "I spy /s/ /ō/ /p/. It is something you use to wash your hands. What do I spy?" (soap)

ACTIVITY 2: Small, Medium, Huge
Skill: Oral Segmentation

Using the picture cards on pages 70–71, or pictures cut out from magazines, display two pictures. Ask children to count how many sounds they hear in each picture name. Then have children select the picture whose name has the most sounds. For example, if the two pictures are _pie_ and _cat_, the children would count two sounds for _pie_ (/p/ /ī/) and three sounds for _cat_ (/k/ /a/ /t/). They would then choose _cat_, because it has more sounds. Continue with the following picture sets.

- tie (2), sun (3)
- leaf (3), bee (2)
- lock (3), clock (4)
- soap (3), snake (4)
- tie (2), six (4)

When children become skilled at this, increase the number of pictures to three.

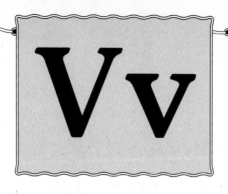

Vacuum Cleaner
by Ethel Jacobson

The vacuum cleaner
Goes vvv, vvv, vvvv.
It vacuums the rugs,
The sofas and chairs,
Beneath the piano,
And up the stairs.
Vvv, vvv, vvvv,
Around the TV.
If I don't move
It might vacuum me!
Vvv, vvv, vvvvv!

Phonemic Awareness Songs and Rhymes   Scholastic Professional Books, 1999

Learning with the Poem

**To focus on the /v/ sound, follow the Instructional Routine on page 7.
Then select one or both of the following activities.**

ACTIVITY 1: Music Center
Skill: Sound Perception

Create a music center in your classroom. Fill the center with recordings of popular rhymes and songs. In addition, locate recordings of environmental sounds such as vrooming vacuum cleaners, honking horns, chirping birds, or mooing cows. Have children listen to the sounds and match them to pictures of each object or animal. These and other playful activities will help children focus on and identify sounds in their environment and language.

ACTIVITY 2: Clean Up!
Skill: Oddity Task

Make a set of Clean Up! game cards using the following picture cards on pages 70–71: *bat, ball, can, cat, dog, duck, fan, fish, gate, goat, leaf, log, man, mop, nest, nine, pan, pig, sock, sun, ten, top*. This game is played just like Go Fish, except children are to match picture cards whose names begin with the same sound. When a player doesn't have a card with the requested initial sound, he or she says "Clean Up!" instead of "Go Fish!" Each player begins with five cards.

Willoughby Wallaby Woo

by Dennis Lee

Willoughby Wallaby Wee
An elephant sat on me.
Willoughby Wallaby Woo
An elephant sat on you.

Willoughby Wallaby Wustin
An elephant sat on Justin.
Willoughby Wallaby Wanya
An elephant sat on Tanya.

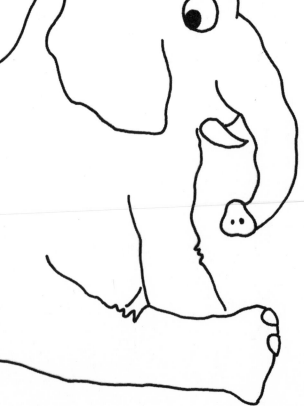

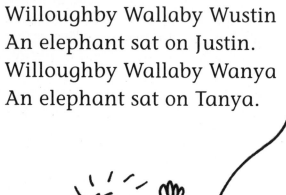

Phonemic Awareness Songs and Rhymes Scholastic Professional Books, 1999

Learning with the Poem

**To focus on the /w/ sound, follow the Instructional Routine on page 7.
Then select one or both of the following activities.**

ACTIVITY 1:
Willoughby Wallaby Who?
Skill: Phonemic Manipulation

Use the last portion of "Willoughby Wallaby Woo" when taking attendance or lining up children for recess. For example, you might say "Willoughby Wallaby Wustin, Let's line up _____." (Justin) Have the class provide the correct student name.

ACTIVITY 2: Switch and Find
Skill: Phonemic Manipulation

Display the following picture cards from pages 70–71: *bat, cat, hat, boat, coat, goat, can, man, fan, pan, lock, sock, mop, top.* Select one picture card. Then tell children that you will say a sound. You want them to replace the first sound in the picture name with the sound you state, and find the picture card whose name is the new word formed. For example, choose the *lock* picture card, say /s/, and help children find the *sock* picture card. Continue with the following cards and clues:

CARD	CLUE	ANSWER
bat	/k/	(cat)
mop	/t/	(top)
man	/f/	(fan)
boat	/g/	(goat)
coat	/b/	(boat)
pan	/k/	(can)

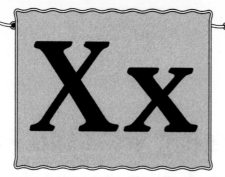

Xx

Chicken Pox
by Terry Cooper

I've got the
itchy
itchy
scratchy
scritchy
head-to-socks
drive-me-crazy
chicken pox.

64

Learning with the Poem

**To focus on the /ks/x sounds, follow the Instructional Routine on page 7.
Then select one or both of the following activities.**

ACTIVITY 1: Box It
Skill: Oral Segmentation

Place two picture cards (see pages 70–71) on a desk. Be sure that the picture names contain a different number of sounds. For example, use the picture cards for *sock* (3 sounds) and *tie* (2 sounds) from page 71. Then place a set of blocks on the table, the number of blocks corresponding to the number of sounds in one of the picture card names. Ask children to select the picture card whose name contains that number of sounds. If necessary, model for children how to segment each picture card name by stretching out the word and moving one block for each sound heard.

ACTIVITY 2: Scratch It
Skill: Oral Segmentation, Oral Blending

Tell children that they are going to pretend they have the itchy, itchy, scratchy, scritchy chicken pox from head to toe. To help get rid of the itching, you will teach them a special exercise. You will say a word—stretching each sound in the word. The children are to put their hands on their head for the first sound, their waist for the second sound, and their toes for the third sound as they stretch the word. Then they are to say the word at a natural pace. Use these and other three-phoneme words: *got, sock, leg, head, sick, nice.*

Then tell children that you will say a word that contains /ch/ as in *chicken*. If they hear the /ch/ sound at the beginning of the word, they are to touch their head. If they hear /ch/ in the middle of the word, they are to touch their waist. If they hear /ch/ at the end of the word, they are to touch their toes. Use these and other words: *children, chance, scratch, itch, chicken, watching, patches, chop, latch.*
Continue with other sounds and words.

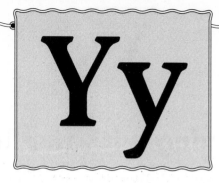

If You're Happy and You Know It

If you're happy and you know it,
Clap your hands.
If you're happy and you know it,
Clap your hands.
If you're happy and you know it,
Then your face will surely show it.
If you're happy and you know it,
Clap your hands.

If you're happy and you know it,
Blink your eyes.
If you're happy and you know it,
Blink your eyes.
If you're happy and you know it,
Then your face will surely show it.
If you're happy and you know it,
Blink your eyes.

Phonemic Awareness Songs and Rhymes   Scholastic Professional Books, 1999

Learning with the Song

To focus on the /y/ sound, follow the Instructional Routine on page 7.
Then select one or both of the following activities.

ACTIVITY 1: Sound It Out
Skill: Oral Blending, Oral Segmentation

Write the song "Sound It Out" on chart paper. Sing the song to the tune of "If You're Happy and You Know It." At the end of the song, say a word in parts for children to orally blend. For example, /y/...ellow or /y/ /e/ /s/. Then sing the song several times. At the end of each singing, point to a child to provide word parts for the class to blend.

Sound It Out
If you have a new word, sound it out.
If you have a new word, sound it out.
If you have a new word,
Then slowly say the word.
If you have a new word, sound it out.

ACTIVITY 2: Sing a Song of Sounds
Skill: Oral Segmentation

Write the song "If" on chart paper. Sing it to the tune of "If You're Happy and You Know It." During each singing, replace /y/ with a different sound. Use common beginning sounds of students' names such as /s/, /m/, /t/, and /p/. You might also wish to replace "clap your hands" with movements such as stand up, touch your head, or hop around.

If
If your name begins with /y/, clap your hands,
If your name begins with /y/, clap your hands,
If your name begins with /y/, clap your hands and say your name,
If your name begins with /y/, clap your hands.

As a variation, have children use picture cards with the song. Have them clap their hands when their picture card name's first sound is sung. You might also wish to replace "begins" with "ends" to focus on final sounds.

Zz

Zip, Zoom

Zip, Zoom,
Zip, Zoom,
Zip, Zoom,
The buzzing bee
Flew through my room.
Zip, Zee,
Zip, Zee,
Zip, Zee,
It flew out the window
And up the tree.
Zip,
Zoom,
Zee!

Phonemic Awareness Songs and Rhymes Scholastic Professional Books, 1999

Zz

Learning with the Poem

To focus on the /z/ sound, follow the Instructional Routine on page 7.
Then select one or both of the following activities.

ACTIVITY 1:
Zip, Zoom—Find Your Match!
Skill: Oddity Task

Make picture card necklaces using large index cards and the picture cards from pages 70–71. You and your students may even want to illustrate some cards of your own. Punch holes in the top two corners of each card and string a piece of yarn through them to create a picture card necklace. Distribute one card to each child. Have children "zip around the room" to find their match by finding the classmates whose picture card begins with the same sound, ends with the same sound, or rhymes (depending on the skill you are working on).

ACTIVITY 2: Sound Switcheroo
Skill: Phonemic Manipulation

Explain to children that you want them to listen carefully to the sounds in the word you're going to say. Tell them that you'll then play switcheroo (change one sound in the word—the beginning, middle, or ending sound) with one of these sounds. Children should then tell you which sound was switched. For example, if you say *zip* and then *lip*, children should respond that /z/ was switched with /l/. Continue with these and other word pairs:

- zap/tap
- fan/fat
- zig/pig
- pick/pack
- pig/pin
- gate/game
- van/ran
- cup/cap
- run/sun
- zag/rag
- hat/hot
- leaf/loaf
- fish/dish
- zoom/room
- hot/hop
- tap/tape

Picture Cards

Phonemic Awareness Songs and Rhymes Scholastic Professional Books, 1999

Picture Cards

Bibliography

Books with Rhyme

Bears in Pairs by N. Yektai (Bradbury, 1987)

Bears on the Stairs: A Beginner's Book of Rhymes by M. & L. Kalish (Scholastic, 1993)

Buzz Said the Bee by W. Lewison (Scholastic, 1992)

Carrot/Parrot by J. Martin (Simon & Schuster, 1991)

Catch a Little Fox by Fortunata (Scholastic, 1968)

Chicken Soup with Rice by M. Sendak (Scholastic, 1962)

Each Peach Pear Plum by J. and A. Ahlberg (Puffin Books, 1986)

Father Fox's Pennyrhymes by C. Watson (Scholastic, 1987)

A Giraffe and a Half by S. Silverstein (HarperCollins, 1964)

Hop on Pop by Dr. Seuss (Random House, 1987)

Hunches in Bunches by Dr. Seuss (Random House, 1982)

The Hungry Thing by J. Slepian and A. Seidler (Scholastic, 1988)

I Can Fly by R. Krauss (Western Publishing, 1992)

Is Your Mama a Llama? by D. Guarino (Scholastic, 1992)

It Does Not Say Meow and Other Animal Riddle Rhymes by B. Schenk de Regniers (Houghton Mifflin, 1972)

Jamberry by B. Degen (Harper & Row, 1983)

Miss Mary Mack and Other Children's Street Rhymes by J. Cole and S. Calmenson (Morrouno, 1990)

101 Jump-Rope Rhymes by J. Cole (Scholastic, 1989)

Pickle Things by M. Brown (Parents Magazine Press/Putnam & Grosset, 1980)

The Random House Book of Poetry for Children (Random House, 1983)

See You Later Alligator... by B. Strauss and H. Friedland (Price Stern Sloan, 1986)

Sheep in a Jeep by N. Shaw (Houghton Mifflin, 1986)

Sing a Song of Popcorn by B. Schenk de Regniers, M. White, and J. Bennett (Scholastic, 1988)

Street Rhymes Around the World by J. Yolen (Wordsong, 1992)

Yours Till Banana Splits: 201 Autograph Rhymes by J. Cole and S. Calmenson (Beech Tree, 1995)

Books with Alliteration

A, My Name is Alice by J. Bayer (Dial, 1994)

All About Arthur (an absolutely absurd ape) by E. Carle (Franklin Watts, 1974)

Alphabears by K. Hague (Henry Holt, 1984)

Animalia by G. Base, (Abrams, 1987)

Aster Aardvark's Alphabet Adventures by S. Kellogg (Morrow, 1987)

Busy Buzzing Bumblebees and Other Tongue Twisters by A. Schwartz (Harper & Row, 1982)

Dinosaur Chase by C. Otto (HarperCollins, 1993)

Dr. Seuss's ABC by Dr. Seuss (Random House, 1963)

Faint Frogs Feeling Feverish and Other Terrifically Tantalizing Tongue Twisters by L. Obligade (Viking, 1983)

Six Sick Sheep: 101 Tongue Twisters by J. Cole and S. Calmenson (Beech Tree, 1993)

Tongue Twisters by C. Keller (Simon & Schuster, 1989)

Zoophabets by R. Tallon (Scholastic, 1979)

Books with Phonemic Manipulation

The Cow That Went Oink by B. Most (Harcourt, 1990)

Don't Forget the Bacon by P. Hutchins (Morrow, 1976)

There's a Wocket in My Pocket by Dr. Seuss (Random House, 1989)

Zoomerang a Boomerang: Poems to Make Your Belly Laugh by C. Parry (Puffin Books, 1993)

**For additional books, see "Read-Aloud Books for Developing Phonemic Awareness: An Annotated Bibliography" by Hallie Kay Yopp in *The Reading Teacher*, Vol. 48, No. 6, March 1995.

References

Adams, M. J. 1990. *Beginning to Read: Thinking and Learning About Print.* Cambridge: Massachusetts Institute of Technology.

Ball, E. W., and B. A. Blachman. 1991. "Does Phoneme Awareness Training in Kindergarten Make a Difference in Early Word Recognition and Developmental Spelling?" *Reading Research Quarterly* 26 (1).

Blevins, W. 1998. *Phonics from A to Z: A Practical Guide.* New York: Scholastic.

Blevins, W. 1997. *Phonemic Awareness Activities for Early Reading Success.* New York: Scholastic.

Juel, C., P. Griffith, and P. Gough. 1986. "Acquisition of Literacy: A Longitudinal Study of Fifty-Four Children from First Through Fourth Grades." *Journal of Educational Psychology* 80.

Shankweiler, D., and I. Liberman. 1989. *Phonology and Reading Disability: Solving the Reading Puzzle.* Ann Arbor: University of Michigan Press.

Snider, V. E. 1995. "A Primer on Phonemic Awareness: What It Is, Why It's Important, and How to Teach It." *School Psychology Review* 24 (3).